There's Something About Him

There's Something About Him

TANYA DENISE

Writer's Block Press
www.writersblockpress.com

Printed in the United States of America

First Printing, June 2024

"The best relationships are the ones you don't see coming."

From our playlist:
"Naked" by Ella Mai

To the man who stood out...

To the man who was clear, direct, expressive,
and intentional...
Just like I prayed.

To the man who was sure about himself
and sure about me...

To the man who inspired me and gave me hope,

To the man who pierced & captured my heart.

C.D. aka (my) CLuv,
This is for you.

XOXO,
Luvface

From our playlist:
"Crush" by Yuna w/ Usher

Contents

An Answered Prayer

I cried myself to sleep that night. Before I dozed off, I was praying. I was hurt. I was tired.

I begged God to sever anything in me towards someone who had been in my life for years, yet nothing ever became of it. When I say *nothing* became of it, I mean he never stepped to the plate to take things to the next level. I cared about this person deeply; however, we were never in a committed relationship. I was tired of wondering, tired of waiting, tired of hoping, and tired of trying to figure things out. I wanted more. I deserved more. *More* is what I asked God for.

Curled up in my bed, crying my heart out, I asked God to send someone who would meet me where I was and be willing to grow with me. I asked God for a man who was direct, expressive, and intentional. I asked for a man who was sure of himself and sure about me.

I need a man with integrity, values, morals,

boundaries, discipline, and self-control. I prayed for someone who could and would express how he felt. Someone who was not afraid of his feelings. Someone who was clear and expressive about life, about the world, about love, and about me. I prayed for someone who wasn't afraid to take a chance on love, *the real kind*. I desired someone who was transparent and focused; someone ready for a healthy, lasting relationship, and someone who would lead the relationship and eventually lead me (as the head).

I desired to be matched with my purpose partner. The man who I naturally complimented, by design. The man who valued my gift(s), my input, my opinion, and my purpose in his life, and in the world. A man who was not threatened by me, my goals, and my ambition. A man who was inspired by all of it instead. A man with vision and a man who was ready to execute purpose together, plus prepare, provide, and protect in the process.

I knew my worth and value. I knew what I brought to the table. I understand my role and position as a woman, and I know that I am somebody's wife.

I was more specific than I had ever been in that prayer. I poured my heart out that night. I had loved and lost before. My picker was not good, so I asked God to pick for me. I had very specific terms in mind. Consistency was huge. Making me a priority was important. A man of action was necessary.

The next day, I joined a dating site. I was not *looking* for a relationship, despite the prayer. I was positioning myself, however. I assumed God would need time to put together the masterpiece I prayed for. My request was very detailed. In fact, I was slightly doubting the availability or the existence of the man I described in my prayer. I know God can do *anything*; however, I was honestly unsure about there being a man who would fit the mold I had come up with.

I had been with men who were emotionally unavailable. I had been with men who were unhealed and unwilling to do the work. I had settled for situationships one too many times and found myself fighting for a commitment. I knew that wasn't right and eventually it got old. I had been married and divorced. I was losing hope where relationships, commitment, and true love were concerned.

I wanted genuine commitment. I wanted companionship. I had had enough of brunch with the girls and traveling with my mother. Don't get me wrong, I enjoyed all of that and still do, however I wanted to do those things with *my* man. My sons were more interested in their friends and their personal interests at their ages and rightfully so. It was time for me to have *my* person and enjoy a healthy relationship.

I did not want a fling or anything casual. I desired marriage just not right away. I wanted my lifetime and my lovetime, *my* person, *my* guy.

That evening, on the dating app, I matched with five men. That was my max. From past experience, I knew they'd eventually weed themselves out and I'd be recruiting for the five-star list again, unless I became disgusted with the experience as before.

I hated the dating process. I disliked online dating. Weeding men out was like going through a stack of applications of unqualified candidates. It was no fun at all. Most of the "applicants" never made it past the dating app.

I had promised my sister, Tiana, that I would give it two weeks this time. The last time I barely made it 48 hours. It takes a lot of patience to date in general. Online dating is a beast of its own.

There I was swiping through the profiles of the first five. *He* was one of the first that I matched with. When I saw his picture, the first thing I noticed was his smile. He has an amazing smile! It was coy, yet genuine, calm, and inviting.

He was wearing a blue, long-sleeved, button-down dress shirt and a tie. I loved his presentation. He had dark skin and a bald head. Ask my mama and my sister, Trina, about me and a bald head, especially a chocolate one! *Lord, have mercy*!

There was something about him. I smiled at his picture and began reading his profile. He was 6'2" (good God almighty) and he was looking for a long-term relationship (okay, okaaay). He had a sense of humor based on his write-up. Most guys did not write much of anything and those who did were not good at spelling. That was a turn off.

C.D. could spell. That was a turn on. In his write up, he pointed out the importance of communication, and setting life goals. I studied communication and not only did I set life goals, but I usually set annual and monthly goals, sometimes weekly and daily goals, too. I can't recall reading a profile before this one where the man talked about goal setting. *Who was this guy?*

His initial contact was simple and subtle. He was polite and respectful, too. He complimented one of my photos and I sent a thank you. That's it. I was not interested in taking the lead in any way. To my surprise, he responded and initiated a chat conversation. (I positioned myself, he approached and gently nudged. I responded and remained positioned, then he took another step. See how this works?)

He told me that he had read my profile, and he was interested in getting to know more about me. He asked me to tell him about myself, however I told him to go first. I was guarded as I should have been. I was not expecting much at all. I refused to waste my time and ability to communicate on someone who was unable to communicate. So, the spotlight was on him.

To my surprise again, C.D. was on it. His communication was on point. He responded and provided information about himself very openly. He told me about where he grew up, his parents, his children, his job, his interests – he covered a lot in a brief period. He even alluded to things I had mentioned in my profile, to make sure that I knew he read it. Clever! He was detailed, clear, and engaging.

I am a word person. I am a writer and a speaker. I am a texter and a reader. So, when he sent lengthy, detailed messages, and shared so much, I was intrigued.

After three days on the dating app, two of the "first five applicants" had already weeded themselves out. My inbox was full of unqualified guys who made my head hurt. I was ready to delete the app.

C.D. had my attention and interest, even with two other pursuers (who eventually fell off). He sent another detailed and lengthy message. He had me smiling and laughing out loud, which was not easy to do.

We had an effective communication thread going. He closed his message with a song dedication, and it was a song on my playlist. Imagine that! I replied with my telephone number. He called me that evening and we talked for more than two hours.

I PRAYED...

For a man who is AWARE.
Aware of himself.
Where he is.
Where he's been.
Where he's going.
What he needs.
What he desires.
How he feels.
A man aware...
Of the value of woman.
Who she is.
What she brings.
And his need for her.

I prayed...

For a man who is CLEAR.
About himself.
About his future.
About his intentions.
About his feelings.
About his purpose.
About his goals.
About me.

I prayed...

For a man with VISION.
The ability to see what others don't see.
The ability to see and create with his mind.
The ability to see what is and what will be.
The ability to see me...
A man with foresight and a plan.

I prayed...

For a man who is READY.
To commit to me.
To be honest with me.
To be faithful to me.
To lead me.
To cover me.
To love...me.
To protect...
The most fragile and delicate parts of me
(my heart, my dreams, my purpose).

I prayed...

For a man who PROVIDES.
A safe space for me.
Security for my heart.
Shelter from the harshness of the world.
Arms strong enough to hold & lift me up.
A man who would provide guidance, counsel,
care, and correction- all for my protection.

I prayed...
For a man who is sure about himself
And sure about me.
One who is in tune with how he feels and
comfortable expressing his feelings to me and
about me.

A man who will love me out loud,
Someone proud to call me his.
A man who likes to hold my hand and kiss it.
A man hungry for my embrace,
One who loves the taste of my lips.

I prayed...
For a man who accepts me,
Someone I compliment,
Someone who supports me to no end,
Someone to balance me,
And compliment me, too.

I prayed...
For a man who could touch me...
Without touching me.
A man who would love me, naked....
With clothes on.
A man who isn't in a rush...
and values taking his time...with me.

I prayed for a man who adores me!!
A man who looks at me with deep appreciation.

A man who touches my face, plays in my hair,
kisses me while I'm asleep,
And pulls me close at night.

A man who isn't afraid to look deeply into my
eyes. A man who inhales my scent, and exhales
love that saturates my being.

I prayed for a man who won't mind becoming my
best friend, sharing time, space, and energy as
partners & lovers. A man who safely trusts in me
enough to be vulnerable. A man who isn't afraid
to allow me to be & fill in the missing rib,
help guard his heart, while honoring his manhood
with gratitude and respect.

I prayed... for the man for me...*my* man, *my* lover,
my friend, *my* partner, *my* covering....
Because I don't want someone who belongs to
anyone else,
Physically, mentally, emotionally, or spiritually.

I prayed....

He Kissed Me

C.D. was easy to talk to. From the moment the first call connected, we clicked. It was natural, or in his words "organic."

He had a sense of humor and kept a smile on my face. He knew how to keep the conversation going. We bounced around touching on several topics. It was a refreshing phone call, and it did not seem like it was the first time we had talked.

He was down to earth, easy going, and intelligent. He was knowledgeable about many things. He took interest in history, international news, and business. I was impressed with the quality of our conversation.

We had a lot in common and in the areas where we were different, there was respectful discussion and understanding. I was captivated by CD's voice and my mind was blown by the flow of the conversation. *There was something about him*!

C.D. and I would talk by phone, daily, for a minimum of two hours. The longest phone call was logged at eight and a half hours. We were putting in work and time. I have receipts!

When I say that we spent a lot of time together, I mean every bit of that. We sent text messages in between phone calls, sharing pictures, thoughts, and ideas. We talked and laughed to great lengths. We talked about so many things. From parenting, to politics, romantic relationships, friendships, business, religion, health, cooking, finances, music, and much more. Things flowed so *organically*.

We were on the phone one evening and he told me that he was going to be in my area. We lived more than 200 miles apart. He had connections my way, so I assumed he was coming to town on business.

"Are you coming to see your folks and adding me to the agenda?" I asked.

"No, I am coming to see *you*, and if time permits I will add my folks to the agenda," he responded.

A week later, he showed up in the middle of the day (as planned). When he arrived to pick me up, I was wearing a long, sleeveless, colorful dress with a cardigan (always a lady). He had on shorts and a complimentary top.

He stepped out of his special edition Ford truck, and I smiled. Standing in front of me was a masterpiece! Hershey chocolate skin, tall, dark, and handsome, to say the least. He was a fine specimen of a man! We exchanged hellos and briefly hugged.

We had planned to go share a bite to eat. When I asked where we should go, he suggested Mexican food and stated that he knew it was my favorite. *He remembered*. I was flattered.

We went to one of my favorite restaurants, had lunch, drinks, enjoyable conversation and lots of laughs. After so many hours of phone calls, being in person was natural and comfortable for us.

From across the table, C.D. looked at me, sipped his drink, and said, "You know you're off the market, right?"

I giggled.

"I really don't see anything funny," he sarcastically replied.

Did I mention that he had a sense of humor and kept me laughing? I giggled again as I sipped my drink. What he didn't know is that I had deleted my profile from the dating app before we got to the restaurant. *I know, I know*. Tiana told me to give it a week. I promised to give it two weeks and I did just that.

I liked C.D. already. *I know, I know*. It was still very early; however, we had spent a significant amount of time already talking. Plus, I had been praying. I felt peace about this.

I was just fine to be friends with him because we vibed really well. I enjoyed talking to him and wanted to continue getting to know him. I didn't want the distraction of other men trying to impress me. My focus was not a relationship at that moment; however, I was open to the possibility, especially after C.D. naturally spoke on the very things I had prayed about.

During the many phone conversations, he spoke about consistency, making his lady a priority, and it had only been a few weeks, however I liked how he moved. He was on point, and he didn't miss a beat. He shared what he desired in life and in a long term, committed relationship. It was exactly what I desired. It seemed too good to be true.

I did not tell him what I wanted initially. I let him do most of the talking. I listened intently and I paid attention to what he said compared to what he did. I took everything back to God, in prayer.

Let me insert that I am not super religious. I am an imperfect woman of faith who believes in a perfect God. I believe in the Bible and the power of prayer. I had made many mistakes before in life and when it came to relationships. I didn't want to repeat the cycle, hence the reason I saturated this experience in prayer.

When C.D. inquired about what I was looking for, I explained to him that I was not looking. I told him that I wanted him to just be himself and I needed to be myself. If we were a match, then we'd know, but if I gave him a cheat sheet on what I wanted it would be easy for him to become that versus just being who he was. I needed to see and know who he was.

I was sitting in my seat across from him at the restaurant. He got up from his seat, walked around to my seat and came close. The way he looked at me and leaned in I thought something was wrong with my face.

He gently lifted my chin, leaned down, and he kissed me on my lips. Once... twice... and three times. Slow. Soft. Gentle.

My body was flooded with warmth and nervousness. I was not a kisser - at all. I mean, I did not like to kiss, and I wasn't an affectionate person. In the moment, I did not know if I was offended by the kisses... or if I liked them.

He returned to his seat, sat back, and looked at me. I sipped my drink while blushing and the more I gave it thought I realized I liked his kisses. I could still feel his lips on mine, and I wanted more but there was no way I was going to tell him that. In fact, I was still processing what had happened.

By the time we met in person, I already determined that I liked this guy. He liked me, too. It was early, I know. I'm just saying.

He spent his off day from work driving from Las Vegas, Nevada, to Redlands, California, to meet me. That meant a lot to me. The night before he arrived, we video chatted for the first time. It was cute because as much as we talked by telephone, when the cameras were on, all we could do was smile and laugh for the first hour. Once the ice was broken, we found ourselves in bed, holding our phones, looking at one another, and smiling. It was cheesy yet sweet. The video chat eased any anxiety about meeting in person.

***

After the late lunch, C.D. and I headed to Newport Beach. The drive down was filled with listening to the music we had shared with one another over the prior two weeks. We had an entire playlist of songs that he sent to me and songs that I sent to him. We also had a brief conversation while on the road. The time together felt good. He held my hand while driving and when he needed both hands to navigate the vehicle, my hand rested on his leg. We were comfortable with one another, organically.

When we arrived at the beach, he came around to my side of the vehicle and opened my door. That's a requirement for me. I shared that with him during one of the many phone calls. He was careful to be a gentleman and I loved every bit of it.

Before I could get out of the truck, he leaned in and kissed me, again.

"Another one?!" I said as I blushed.

"Oh, don't act like you don't like it," he said.

I giggled. He was right. I liked it and I liked him.

"You're going to be craving these kisses one day. Watch!" He said with much confidence.

I giggled, again.

He was right and it wasn't long before I was the kiss initiator. I found myself going in for a kiss a few times and of course he was receptive. These were not passionate kisses, yet they were intimate, gentle, intentional, and spoke words of their own.

We walked along the beach without shoes, hand in hand. The water was cold and so was the sand. There was a beautiful, colorful sunset that evening. We took pictures and just enjoyed one another. It was sweet and romantic. Everything about being with him felt right.

At one point, he walked up and embraced

me. For someone who wasn't affectionate, it felt good to be in his arms. His profile said he was 6'2", however I stood on my tippy toes to kiss him and could have sworn he stood 6'4". He was thin, with an athletic build, strong, yet gentle. So, when he wrapped his arms my 5'9" plus sized body, it was a treat. He held me tight, and he held me right. I especially enjoyed looking up to him and gazing into his eyes.

By sunset, I kissed him several more times. He told me that I was going to crave his kisses one day and he was right. I craved his kisses, his hugs, his touch, and him the rest of that day and for the duration of our relationship.

HE KISSED ME

Oh my gosh, how could this be?

He looked into my eyes, then he kissed me.

He lifted my chin, drew close to my face,

He took a step closer and was all in my space!

His lips touched mine, my head started to spin,

I thought that was it until he leaned back in.

He kissed me again, his lips melted into mine,

I thought he was done, til he kissed me a third time.

When he stepped back, he took my breath away.

So many thoughts filled my mind,

Yet no words I could say.

He kissed me....

Like no one I've ever known,

My heart became putty,

And his heart became my home.

From our playlist:
"For Real" by Amel Larrieux

LOVE NOTE #1

To: You
From: Me

If you have not figured it out yet, I am a highly emotional person. I feel very intensity and passion. I often express myself in the same manner.

Because I am "open" in this new space with you, my emotional capacity has been triggered. I'm thinking. I'm seeing. I'm feeling.

What tends to happen is the emotions multiply and overflow. When they do, I have to release them and my most common method is writing, so here I am...

I'm in my bed. I should be asleep, but I'm covered

in the after effect of our time together.

First, let me acknowledge the joy I felt seeing your name on my phone screen last night. I like to hear from you, and I look forward to it.

Then, let's point out the excitement and comfort I experienced once I heard your voice... An instant smile took my face hostage. Your voice resonates with me. I like hearing you speak and as I have said before I love how expressive you are. I also like that when we disagree on an idea, a thought, or anything, it's not a disagreement- it's just an open space of respected shared ideas and thoughts.

It's not easy getting off the phone with you. I don't know if that's good or bad yet. I can talk with you for hours as we have been.

I listen to your words intently. My mind and my heart have a scanner and certain things stand out. I highlight them and file them... subconsciously.

I can't say "I've heard that before," with the words you express. A few things are familiar sounding, however what you say and how you say it coupled with the sincerity of your heart causes me to pause. The more you pour, the more I collect and my respect for you grows.

Your words replay in mind throughout the day. It's funny how easily we both share and exchange words by phone. Then, when we saw one another LIVE on camera, some sort of shyness kicked in. We weren't as fluid in our conversation with the camera on, however the smiles said a lot and we both warmed up well. I think that camera call broke the ice a bit which made Monday a breeze.

You are my new interest and inspiration. I am digging you. 🥰 I love our good morning text messages and daily song dedications. I look forward to waking up to see a message from you. I don't know what the future holds but I'm living in the moment. In the moment, I'm in my feelings, in a positive and good way as this story unfolds.

In the moment, you've got my attention and there's an attraction I have never felt or experienced before you. It excites me....and it scares me...just a bit.

I admire your desire for a close partner who you can dote on, serve, and protect. I wonder if you can pull off the vision you have... because I can see myself as part of it. I wonder if you can handle the many layers of me and my heart. I wonder if the things we haven't shared yet will be accepted and understood once we go there.

I wonder if the distance between us will serve us well or at some point become too much. I wonder what God had in mind when He approved the part of our life's journey that said we'd cross paths and on August 29th we'd connect.

Now here we are with the reality of what seems like an opportunity that we both have been praying for.

LOVE NOTE #2

Hello, my Hershey kisses chocolate pudding muffin! 😚🥰💕

You said yesterday that I have a sweet tooth, well you are my indulgence! 💖

Surprisingly, I like the feel of your lips against mine and I love being in your arms!! That first kiss at the restaurant caught me off guard. I was a little uncomfortable, yet I digested the discomfort and discovered that I liked how it felt. That was a shock to me because what I told you is no lie. I did not enjoy kissing prior to you, prior to this. It all feels so natural or organic as you'd say.

Your hugs feel amazing. The extended hug edition at the beach was everything! I fell in love with being wrapped in your arms at that moment!

All of this is a sweet surprise. You showed up right after I prayed, and you've shown me that everything I petitioned God for is more than possible. We're still learning about each other and still feeling things out...but I think we've hit the jackpot!

As I have expressed before, I'm not here to play games. I'm not here to hurt you. I don't believe you are here to play games or to hurt me. We have established that we both want something different than what we have had before and I'm confident that we have everything we need to create that very thing.

XOXO

Taking The Lead

C.D. was intentional. Just like I prayed. He was aware of what he wanted, where he had been, and where he was going. He was transparent and honest. He was direct and expressive, just like I prayed.

When he missed me, he did not hesitate to say so. I like that. When he took a liking to me, he made sure that I knew. I needed that. When he wanted to talk with me, he called. And he called often. When he wanted to see me, he let me know so we could make plans. He was clear about his intentions and that was a turn on.

Let me be clear about the fact that we were attracted to one another and very respectful. He did not grope me or attempt to touch me inappropriately at any point. That should be obvious, however I had been on dates where men had no self-control or respect. Sex was introduced in conversation by them way too early. There was something about C.D. He was different. He wanted more. He showed me something different with every passing moment.

C.D. was active and engaging. He was clear and he was open. He told me things that he didn't have to tell me at this juncture. It created a space of trust and respect.

I was flattered when he told me that he told his mother about me. He had also told his sister and a buddy or two about me. I had done the same thing by sharing with those close to me that I had met someone wonderful.

We were 44 and 53 years old in a very positive space of getting to know one another and moving in an agreeable direction. A month passed quickly and although we lived 236 miles apart, we both made a point of seeing one another regularly. We spent a lot of time together and it was easy.

C.D. led us from acquaintances to dating, then from just dating to dating exclusively. It wasn't long after becoming exclusive that he initiated the next level of courting or a committed relationship. I did not have to ask what we were or where we were going. He took the lead every step of the way. I loved it and I needed that.

He invited me to travel with him for the Christmas holiday to meet his parents and family. He told me that he didn't want to present me as some random woman he was *just dating* to his parents. He wanted them to know that I was someone he was seriously pursuing. These were his words.

I loved the way he initiated conversations about the growth and evolution of the relationship. I loved how intentional and focused he was. In my experience, it was uncommon for men to take the lead in this same manner.

We discussed dating, we discussed exclusivity, we discussed our personal goals and what "long term" meant to us. I was impressed by his leadership in this regard, and I needed to see and experience every bit of it. The way C.D. moved and the way he moved us along was an answered prayer. I had peace and I had joy. My heart was full.

Although I was not looking for a committed relationship when we connected, at my core that is what I desired. I was on the verge of giving up because I started to think the man I desired did not exist. However, this man standing before me said all the right things and he did all of the right things....naturally.....organically.

There was something about him. I was drawn to him from the beginning. In fact, although we didn't make things exclusive right away, I deleted my profile from the dating app prior to our first date because he specifically spoke on things I had prayed about. He was displaying qualities for which I had prayed. No one knew my prayer...besides me and God.

From our playlist:
"Believe" by Raheem DeVaughn

LOVE NOTE #3

Dear CLuv,

Just so you know...I'm all in.

Even in this brief time, and even as we continue to learn, grow, and build, I'm invested here, in you, in us.

You are not an option; you are the priority. The loose ends I had when we met have been tied, gracefully. I appreciate you tying your loose ends as well and thank you for being transparent about it all.

Everyone closest to me knows about you. There's no secret, although I'm also very protective of you and what we're creating.

I know we both have several things outside of one

another to tend to and focus on like business, work, bills, family, friends, hobbies, etc., however feeding the relationship is a priority to me. Quality time together is important to me.

Just so you know, you can call me anytime. You can come over anytime. I've reached a place with you where that access is granted. It's important to me that you have full confidence in me and complete trust. Thank you for granting me the same access. Especially given the distance between us.

It's important to me to connect with you daily, to hear your voice, to know how you are doing, to stay in the loop with the other parts of your life, and to nurture what's developing between us.

Just so you know, YOU are important to me. Your happiness. Your health. Your goals. Your thoughts. Your feelings. Your opinion.

In the time that we've shared, you've shown me so much. I admire so many things about you and I respect you. I'm comfortable with you and have already opened myself in new ways with you. You are receiving a version of me that no man has received because I think you're worth it.

Thank you for being who you are and just know that I'm on a mission to go all the way.

In education, the highest degree is a doctorate and that's when you have exceeded mastery in your field of study. If all goes according to plan, I'm coming for a doctorate level in learning you so that your needs and desires are met & exceeded.

We've been clear about what we want in partnership and love. Between God, the universe, and the powers that be, the opportunity is here and we're dead smack in the middle of it. ❤

From our playlist:
"Wild" by Chris Larocca

LOVE NOTE #4

To: You
From: Me

By now you know that writing is my thing. I have an air of shyness about me; however, I am not afraid to communicate verbally. You and I communicate well and that is great. At the same time, there is still something about expressing myself with written words. So, here I go....

Your presence in my life has pierced my heart. The very thing I wanted to avoid - to protect my heart - has presented itself to me through you. We have established that you are my answered prayer. No matter what. Whether we move forward or not...you are a clear expression of God's answer to my sincere and heartfelt prayer, and I am so grateful.

I did not see any of this coming, but I am not complaining. I am intrigued and attentive to the details of what is unfolding. You stood out from the beginning, and you naturally outshine anyone else who may have had an opportunity to become just a friend. Who you are, based on what I know so far encompasses so much. Not only is my heart pierced but my heart is now open. (Deep breath).

When the heart is open, it is exposed. To be exposed means to be vulnerable. It means one has entered an atmosphere of risk. The risk can be detrimental, or it can be life changing for the better. I am betting on the latter.

Just like you study to pick the weekly wins for football, and you move forward with the team most likely to make your ticket win...in this short period of our time in each other's lives I have decided firmly to move forward with this "team" called "US" that seems highly likely to win. This letter is my petition to you to apply the brakes if you are not fully ready and equipped for the win...for the ride.

The ride could be dangerous if we are not fully ready and equipped. The ride could result in an accident that could have been avoided. The ride may be fun at times and not so much at other times. The ride may have a few twists and turns along the way. But it's a journey worth taking if we are both willing because we are headed in the same direction anyway.

We both expressed being in the position of tying loose ends and clearing out connections that were established before we met. We have both agreed that there is something here and we possess the tools to build from what exists. I feel my heart budding....So, before I let my heart begin the process of getting comfortable I just want to make sure....

Your words replay in my mind throughout the day. Sometimes I am still in awe by the fact of you emphasizing some key things that are extremely important to me. You've gotta be more than amazing to pierce my heart and to outshine others, to cause me to re-evaluate where I am and what I truly desire, and to cause me to cut off the last string of what was a dead situation before you arrived. That alone speaks volumes.

Commitment is important to me. Relationships are important to me. Loyalty, faithfulness, trust, and respect are important to me.

I love love. I love hard. I love long. I love with intensity and passion. So, my love is not for everyone or anyone. Neither is my commitment and loyalty. In fact, like you, I have untouched love. I have parts of me that have been on reserve on purpose waiting for the right man to share with.

I've watched you and I am watching you. I'm listening. I'm paying attention. I may not say anything at times, but sometimes I feel more than I'd like. I'm taking notes. I'm studying you. I tend to be an A student when I study and apply myself. But before I get deep into this curriculum, I am just running it by you again.

Because I think about you all throughout the day. I have literally gone to bed with you on my mind, saw you in my dreams, and woke up with you still on my mind. I am consumed by thoughts of you. Not in a possessive or obsessive way. Not even in a lustful way and I admit that I am physically attracted to you.

I have been praying and the more I pray, the more I feel and the more drawn in I become. I am not super religious either. I used to be. But I do know, value, and appreciate having a relationship with God and consulting God for direction, clarity, confirmation, guidance, wisdom, etc.

I am naturally passionate about the people in my life and the things that matter to me. I can't help but feel...and I feel with great intensity as I mentioned before. No pressure. Just a petition.

So, before I give my heart permission to remain positioned in your direction, I need to hear you say, "It's ok."

An "ok" from you simply reaffirms that my heart can rest here with you and allow trust to continue to build as we move forward to venture into the opportunity we both have to experience something new with one another. An "ok" from you is not restrictive or demanding, it's confirming and comforting, as we navigate what laying the foundation looks like for us and how to build what we desire and need. If it changes, that's okay too, and I simply request that we discuss the change should it come because we both deserve that.

I understand unraveling things of the past sometimes conjures old feelings, and memories and sometimes others are not ready to let go. Sometimes we can't cut them off immediately without it causing an injury that can bleed out. I am fully aware of and respect those kinds of circumstances.

There are also cases where meeting someone new and trying to finally terminate with someone from the past results in an awakened desire to try with the past, even though what's new is still in front of you. That's a tough place to find yourself in. I get it. And should you find yourself there, all I need is for you to talk to me.

If God and life permits, you'll come to find I am extremely easy going, down to earth, understanding, compassionate, flexible, and so much more.

I really like you, CLuv. I did not plan on liking anyone anytime soon. But I'm here now. We're here. My heart is positioned in your direction, open and willing. Is that ok?

Waiting...on your "ok".....

XOXO

YOU

Hearts on fire
You're my desire
Flames are high
I can't deny
How I feel....
I know it's real.
Deal or no deal?
My heart says you
My heart stays true
The love has been easy
So smooth how you please me
Your touch and your kiss
It's you that miss

From our playlist:
"Comfortable" by H.E.R.

By And By

The next few months were filled with a lot of time on the freeway both ways and even airport runs. We continued to see one another weekly, or at least every other week. One-night stays turned into two nights, three nights, four, and five. I went to his place more than he came to mine. At one point, he suggested that I leave a few things at his place for convenience, especially once I start taking flights (to avoid carrying luggage). This was a different level for me, yet I was actively engaged.

C.D. told me early on that he was on a mission to find his person, the woman for him, and he desired to cultivate a relationship like the one his parents had. They had been married over 50 years and from the sounds of it they shared a special love and got along well. We got along well, too. We complimented one another in general and in business.

My sister, Trina, told me I had met my match

when I told her about C.D. She wasn't lying. He was business-minded and so was I. He wasn't dismissive or intimidated by my hustle, like most men. In fact, he was supportive, promoted by projects, and even took off work to show up for one of my biggest events. I showed the same love by doing what I could to add money to his pockets by marketing and promoting his projects as well. The first hustle he told me about, I took it and ran with it. I earned $1,200 for his business in a couple of weeks. We were on a mission.

C.D. was winning in my book. He stood behind me to support my endeavors, put me in front of people to elevate my brand, and he kept a stack of my business cards with him to hand out. He had been sitting on a business venture that I had already jumped on with success. When he found out that I was in the business, we clicked and moved swiftly together to get him in the game, too. Before long, he had surpassed me in the business, and I was super proud of him. I was proud of myself, as well, because I contributed to his growth, elevation, and finances. He put me on, and I put him on. We were a team.

Long before this point, I stopped responding to text messages from the other two guys who made the cut from the dating app. I didn't mean to be rude or disrespectful, however my time, my mind, and my heart were now occupied. I didn't want any distractions and I was interested in really getting to know C.D. and moving forward with him.

I liked him, yet even if we had just established a solid friendship or did business together, I would have accepted that because we vibed really well. I decided early on that I wanted him around. *There was something about him*; I really liked this man!

From the beginning, I told C.D. that I didn't care if he liked me or not. I was not interested in trying to make a good impression or any impression. I let C.D. see the real me from the start. No weave, no eyelashes, total chill mode. I exposed my flaws and my dislikes early on. I needed him to see and know the real me because if he was going to be around on any level I needed to know that he liked the real me and vice versa. I was not willing to change myself to get a man to like me; I was in a place of freedom and acceptance. If he liked me, good for him. If he didn't, oh well. I had been through enough and was tired of trying to prove anything. I needed things to be just as he described.... *organic* and with us it was just that.

***

When C.D. brought up the topic of cohabitation and marriage, I was stunned. We had bypassed the 90-day mark. As mentioned, we talked about many things without hesitation or judgment. Both of us had been married and divorced in the past. We were clear about what we wanted, and we were starting to believe that we had found that in one another. I told him early on that I was not a long-term girlfriend. I was not in a rush to remarry; however, I was not going to be in a relationship with any man for multiple years as a "girlfriend."

We were both very clear about what our relationship goals were, and we agreed to take our time, however we were also feeling confident and sure about our connection. He asked me if I'd be willing to relocate to where he was. I was okay with it. His proposal for me to relocate to another state was actually another answered prayer.

He would send me links to condos and houses. I followed his lead and started sending him places I saw and liked. We'd talk about what we liked or didn't like about the selections. It was a unique way of teaching and learning one another.

We'd screenshot and send links randomly. We started discussing our finances in detail, including calculating the income streams we had to assess an estimated net amount. We did ok individually based on the numbers. Together, we would kill it. Together, we brought in more than a comfortable amount of income that was in alignment with both of our goals personally and professionally. Together, in his words, our quality of life would certainly improve.

The conversations about merging (or moving in together) got real. They were the most mature discussions I had ever had with a man. The reality of our ages, our health, our aging parents, adult children, grandchildren, and other key areas were put on the table. We talked about it. The reality of the possibility of the relationship not working out after merging was also put on the table. We had a plan for all of it. He laid out the plan, I added my two cents, and we had a deal.

One thing he told me that blew my mind was that if we merged and the relationship did not work, he would make sure my son and I were good. He even suggested that if the relationship ended after merging that we should strive to reside in the same home until my son graduated high school to give him a sense of stability until he was out of on his own. Did I tell you that C.D. is a stand-up man?! The respect I have for him is immeasurable.

Based on our numbers and goals, we agreed on an amount to both save in order to plan to merge within the following year. I was stoked. So many layers of my prayer were unfolding in front of me...organically.

C.D.'s leadership skills were impeccable, in our relationship and in business. I felt safe with him. I felt comfortable with him. I trusted him, completely.

He was a man I admired and honored greatly. I watched how he moved, and I liked how he moved. He was responsible and on top of it. He was a man I believed I could trust with my heart. He was a man I believed I could trust to lead me and my teenage son. Plus, the advice he offered my adult son was solid. He was solid!

***

When we traveled out of state to visit his parents, that sealed the deal for me. I mean, I was already sold, however there is something to be said about meeting family. It provides insight into what and who you are dealing with from a different angle.

The fact that he valued me enough to present me to his parents means a lot. We would arrive in another state outside of the one he lived in and the one I lived in, on his mother's birthday and we would depart the day after Christmas. That too was very special to me.

I had a wonderful time with his parents, family, and friends. I had a wonderful time with him being out of town together. Traveling with a partner is one of the many tests that should be taken before getting in too deep because you learn a lot about people when traveling.

I watched C.D. handle unexpected changes in travel plans, I watched him interact with strangers at the airport, on the shuttle bus, etc. I observed him around his family. I watched the reaction and response of his extended family and friends around him. I paid attention to how he treated me around all of them, as well. All of this was new for me, yet it went so well.

It was important to me to feel comfortable

around his folks and of course I wanted to feel welcomed (and I did). I asked C.D. before the trip what would happen if his folks didn't like me. He explained that he was not taking me to meet them for their approval of me. He said that he had already approved, I was his choice, and if they didn't like me that was their problem. Solid – I told you!

Well, there it is. I think they liked me, however. If nothing else, I did feel warmly welcomed by everyone I met. I had peace within and did not feel uncomfortable at any moment.

His parents were especially welcoming. I had a few opportunities to briefly talk with his mother when no one else was around. She gave me a Christmas gift and we exchanged numbers. His pops referred to me as "daughter" and my heart soaked that up, even if he only meant it because of his ministry background.

While in town, C.D. and I went Christmas shopping together. We spent a day out with his parents, his sister, and nephew. We went on a double date with one of his good friends. We visited another one of his good friends and wife who had recently purchased a new home. We went to the casino, went to breakfast and dinner multiple times, ordered pizza in our hotel room, took lots of pictures, and had a fun time. We even wore matching pajamas, which was my idea that he thought was super cheesy, yet he obliged me.

No one could convince me that I had not met *my* person. Did I tell you that *there's something about him*? I was completely smitten. Everything was still fresh and new. We were just approaching six months, however we had never argued or had any real issue, either. We flowed and we fit, even with our differences.

I was not an affectionate person in my relationships before C.D. I'd hold hands but kissing was not my thing, and neither was laying up. With C.D., it was different. I loved holding his hand and hanging onto his arm. I loved it when he kissed me, and I loved kissing him! We'd cuddle on the couch and lay up. Sometimes I fell asleep in his arms or on his chest. I absolutely loved it when he fell asleep in my arms, or in my lap.

In those moments, I rub his back, shoulder, or his bald head and I pray. I love that intimate space of praying over him. It was calming and peaceful for both of us.

Speaking of intimacy, C.D. had more self-control than any man I have known before him. He was a complete gentleman from the beginning. We spent many nights together where he'd hold me in his arms all night...and *just* hold me. The first few times I actually cried as his arms were wrapped around me because I did not know how much I needed to *just* be held.

C.D. touched me with no hands, and he kissed me without lips. Let me be clear about that fact that he's not a soft guy. He's a certified man in every aspect of the word. He's a little rough around the edges and that's necessary, and I like it. But please know there's nothing weak about him.

When he kissed me, it was always slow and gentle. He taught me to kiss without knowing that he was teaching me. Or maybe he knew he was teaching me (Ha!) and I was just open and ready to learn. He taught me a different form of intimacy that I had been longing for. I was comfortable and no longer afraid to let my guard down completely.

I would pray and ask God a question about C.D. Then, he'd call me with the answer. On many occasions I shed tears in thanksgiving to God for the clear and quick answers. C.D. never knew I was shedding tears on the other end of the phone as he spoke to the very prayer I had just prayed. I don't think he knew how much I prayed either.

This man activated a part of me that had been sleeping and was on its death bed. I was losing hope in the kind of love I truly desire. With him, I was inspired in so many ways. He restored my hope.

I naturally enjoyed serving him. I looked forward to implementing ways to make things easier for him. I would make sure he had a hot meal when he got in from work and I'd freshen up the house and myself right before he walked in the door.

I enjoyed cooking for him and finding new, healthy recipes to ensure he was eating right. He cooked for me, and served me, too. We looked out for one another, and it was the little things that mattered so much. He always asked me if I had eaten, and I always asked if he had taken his vitamins. We were good at performing our own wellness checks on one another.

He'd remind me of things I said I needed to do, and I'd remind him of business appointments he had coming up. We had become an integral part of one another's life. I was looking forward to the future we talked about so many times. I was grateful that we got along so well. No arguments. No significant issues. We had regular check-ins to make sure we were happy, and things were intact. He initiated the check-ins, and I loved every bit of it. We just flowed.... organically.

LOVE NOTE #5

CLuv,

I am looking forward to our continued journey with a particular goal in mind! You're my #1 draft, too, and if anyone were to ask I am 'out of stock' 🤣 There is only one new version and it's in your cart so new shoppers can't even see the exclusive opportunity! 🏃 😦

Thank you for sharing time, space, and energy with me. Thank you for being so engaging. Thank you for being a great communicator. Thank you for sending me songs and emojis. Did I tell you how much I love that? 🥰 🥰 ❤️ ❤️ 💛 💛

Thank you for taking the initiative to come to meet me. You could have asked me to come there. You could have asked me to meet you halfway. We could have just kept talking on the phone. You took the initiative and without hesitation and haven't let up! I love that about you! I appreciate your time and sacrifice.

Although we didn't talk as much as we usually do by phone today, I still enjoyed each minute with you.

I miss you already!

LOVE NOTE #6

Mr. C Luv...

I am on my laptop so I can't add all of the cute emojis that I feel would go with my expression to you right now.

I was working, minding my business and you were heavy on my mind, so here I am deviating from my agenda to share a few things with you.

I am smiling as I think about you...

Talking with you penetrated a part of me that was on lock down....our early conversations were intriguing and engaging. You sparked an interest in me that was not there before you came on the scene. The step you took to see me was impactful. It stood out and it made you stand out. Then, we had an enjoyable time together.

I had already taken a liking to you. Our time together when you were in California only added to that. Our time together when I was in Vegas added even more to my love tank.

You are more than a breath of fresh air....you are a gentle flowing breeze. I value and appreciate how well you communicate and express your thoughts, feelings, etc. You're clear about what you desire, what you need, and how you feel. That's so important to me. You're focused and that's important to me. We engage one another and that's important to me.

Your interest in me isn't surface and I like that. It's not all about you when we talk - we both share, we both engage. It's mutual interaction and I like that. I feel comfortable around you and it's easy talking with you. There are so many levels we have yet to explore and if I can be honest I am looking forward to that experience.

I like how we can be in the presence of one another with no words and it's not awkward. I like how we have experienced intimate moments without sexual influence. The way you grab and hold my hand in the car or when we are walking...the way you grab my face and kiss me, over and over. The way you wrap your arms around every inch of my body when we're standing and the way you wrap your body around mine when we are laying down.

You bring a smile to my face and add joy to my life. You make me laugh long after we're off the phone or away from one another. I find myself repeating your words and your jokes in my head. I find myself thinking about you often.

I pray for you, too. Not "for you" as in asking God for you. I pray for your health & well-being. I pray for your peace of mind, innovative ideas and witty inventions activated so you can venture out to do everything you were created to do. I pray for your protection, for your promotion, for your purpose, for provision and increase in your life. I pray for your children and your family. I pray that you walk in wisdom and with major influence. I pray that your discernment is stronger than ever as you navigate life. I pray for nothing less than God's best in every area of your life!

Even if nothing more ever evolved between us, I have enjoyed you and my natural mission is to make a lasting imprint that will add to who you are and who you are becoming. That's not me doubting the possibilities here, it's me releasing all control and guidance to God and making sure

I am treating you as if God handed you to me personally. It's me acknowledging the gift that you are in general.

I am not here to hurt you. I am not here to play games. I am not here to waste your time or mine. I like you Mr.

So far.

I was just desiring a friend and I think I have stumbled upon much more.

Thank you for the time you have shared with me because time is one thing we will never get back. You can make more money, but you can't make more time.

Thank you for sharing your space and energy with me. Thank you for inviting me into your home and trusting me to be in your safe place. Thank you for being bold enough to take a chance with me and on me. I told you I am more than two handfuls. It takes a special man to handle me....and keep me.

Thank you for being affectionate. Although it's the last thing on my list of love languages, I have enjoyed sharing affection with you. In fact, I can't tell you the last time, if ever, that I enjoyed being affectionate. With you, it has just naturally blossomed.

I have peace and that's a good sign. We are both equipped to create something we have never experienced before. Let's keep moving forward and let's make it count! Have a blessed day.

XOXO

From our playlist:
"Practice" by Kayla Rae

THE *REAL* KIND

I used to crave to be madly in love,
So passionately in love,
Lost in love...

I was irrationally in love,
Fastly in love,
Controlled by love,
Blindly in love,
Dangerously in love...
Because it was toxic love.

Determined to stick with it,
Oh, I was sick with it,
Tried hard to get with it,
Movies and R & B with it.

Didn't know what to do,
With this love.
It wasn't cool this love,
I was through with this love.
Needed a new love.

Not madly in love,
Yet gladly in love...
Sanely in love.
Safely in love.

Didn't fall in this love,
Stood tall in this love,
Peaceful in love.
Trusting in love.
Respected in love.
Not neglected in love.

Intimate in love.
Loyal in love.
Saturated in love…
The *real* kind.

LOVE NOTE #7

To: You
From: Me
Date: Wednesday, October 18, 2023
Time: 10:45 pm
Dedication: Can You Stand the Rain by New Edition

You've gracefully become a priority in my life. Moments with you are a highlight each day. There's nothing like sharing time and space together even with no words sometimes. I simply enjoy your presence and the expectation of it. A text. A phone call. Face to face. Even the very thought of you.

You're an answered prayer, a sweet melody recognized by my heart, and a developing safe place for me. I'm comfortable with you, even with my flaws and all. I didn't come to this experience trying to impress you or captivate your interest or attention. I just showed up as me and you showed up as you...now here we are.

You pierced my heart because of the man you are, and you've triggered natural traits inside of me that were dormant before you. I'm inspired by you... the way you think, the way you move, your passion, your goals, and your heart.

It is my honor and pleasure to serve you in ways that offer support to your journey, position, and purpose. It is my joy to pray for you, listen to you, and to consider new ways to make your load lighter...ways to add to you.

I'm captivated by your smile and intrigued with your mind. I'm mesmerized by your kiss, comforted by your touch, and I feel safe in your arms. I'm already proud to claim you, yet still very protective of what's evolving between us.

I'm loving this natural progression of things... like we've been here before when the truth is we're both blessed to be getting a new version of one another...one that no one else has had access to!

I vow to show up fully each day, not based on how I feel but based on the commitment to see this through. To be genuine, pure, honest, and transparent so that you get a clear view... To really see if you were made for me and if I was designed for you. Because everyone should have someone just for them...a safe place to land when they fall, shelter from the storms of life, comfort in difficult moments, support in every endeavor, a voice of reason in the midst of chaos, arms to rest in, lips to kiss, a place to be reaffirmed and validated, uplifted and encouraged, reminded and lovingly checked when needed...a place to peel back the layers, a place to love, share, learn, and grow. A place we create, cultivate, and protect together.

My capacity for love is enormous. I hope you're both ready to receive from it and pour back into it because the flow has been activated! 💜I'm still basking in this weekend. I'm extremely grateful for so much in general and I'm humbled & honored with how things turned out and how they are going.

You, my love, were a highlight of my weekend!! 💜 I really appreciate the sacrifice you made to be there to support me. There were so many little things that you said or did that equate to being big things. Thank you. 😘🙏

Thank you for wanting to be there. Thank you for taking time off work. Thank you for driving. Thank you for attending the event and staying as long as you did. Thank you for the willingness to meet the other important people in my life. Thank you for engaging by taking pictures, conversing with others, etc. There's so much more I can say thank you for. Just know that I hear you, I see you, and I appreciate you. It wouldn't have been the same without you being there. Thank you for showing up and for supporting me. 😘

You are shining so bright in my world, and I am loving every part of it. 💖 *We went to another level this weekend* 🥰 *in more than one way. I'm still wrapped in the passion of it all.* ❤️ *You feel good to every part of me, inside and out, and all in between.*

My heart is open even more now. Just know that my heart is fragile, and I don't do what we've done without thoughtful care and consideration. I have total peace about the progression of things between us and I'm looking forward to everything in store for you and me, as a unit. 💞

With tender love and soft kisses...
Your Lady Luvface
XOXO

The Shift

We spent Valentine's Day together; we spent his birthday together and we had a beautiful time. It was surreal. Although we were all smiles for the celebration, deep in my heart I felt like something was off, however I held my peace.

Two weeks passed. We continued as usual with our daily time by telephone. He came to visit again and as usual we had a wonderful time. We dined in one night with Chinese food and a tv series. We went to the movies the following day in Newport Beach. All was well.

The day that the visit ended, C.D. left my home early in the morning to return to his home. He had to be at work that afternoon and the drive back was more than three hours. Communication waned from the time he left.

He didn't call to let me know he made it back as usual, however we connected later that evening while he was at work. Over the course of the next three days, the phone calls became less frequent, morning and good night text messages were nonexistent, and the nature of our conversations had changed. Something was up.

Call me crazy, however I knew my man. I paid attention to him. I didn't always speak on it, but I was sure to pray on it. We had established a pattern. He moved a certain way. He had a certain energy with me. Something disrupted that.

Suddenly, he was brief and dismissive. He had never been like that with me. When I inquired, he brushed me off. Hmm. It was unlike him. Granted it had only been six months, but C.D. and I spent a lot of time together. A lot. Even when something was going on, he had a tendency to pull me close, to let me in. As he should have, right? Well, not this time.

I prayed for revelation. I also prayed for him because I felt like something wasn't right. In the meantime, I remained available to him, and I maintained my commitment to the business we had.

C.D. was moving differently. Three days turned into a week of weird behavior and broken communication. He was unwilling to talk like before, so I bowed down gracefully. His response and his lack of response to me told me everything I needed to know at the time. I fell back. Completely. He sent a couple of text messages, and he called a time or two. I didn't respond.

***

Six weeks passed. Yep. Six weeks and five days to be exact. The first four weeks were difficult. I could not understand what had happened. We went from talking by phone every day....EVERY DAY....to not talking at all. He went from telling me (almost) everything to me having to question why he didn't tell me this or that! It was weird.

There was an interference of some sort. There was a shift. I felt it and tried to talk with him about it. I wanted him to be open with me like he had always been. Whatever it was threatened the reality we had created. The defenses that protected our union were compromised.

Yes, I am fully aware that six months is no time. It's still a probationary period honestly. But this was not the average love bombing situation. There was no love bombing. We were real and raw with each other, presenting ourselves and not trying to make an impression. He was transparent from the gate so why the sudden change? I have a few theories about what caused the shift, God showed me some things, however it's something me and C.D. have yet to discuss.

I struggled with my feelings over the course of the six and a half weeks. I spent several days in tears, unable to sleep, unable to eat, unable to concentrate on work. I felt myself falling into depression.

I started praying and setting daily goals to pull myself out of the slump. The more I prayed, the more I thought about C.D. and I had dreams about him. One week, I dreamt about him every night. I wanted to shake him off of me completely, because I was still hurt, however *there was something about him*.

I was good at saying goodbye in the past. When I am done, I am done, in every area. In my mind, I was done with C.D., there was nothing to talk about and I didn't plan or expect to see him or talk to him ever again.

I thought about him, of course. I missed him terribly. So many things reminded me of him. He had become an integral part of my life. My schedule had adapted to his. It took a while to come out of the bubble I was in now that he was not around.

I specifically added him to my prayers, which was another thing I didn't normally do. You couldn't pay me to pray for an ex. C.D. was different. My prayers went from asking God to heal my heart, help me to let go, and move on, to inquiring about my original prayer before we met where I thought C.D. was the answer.

I prayed for very specific qualities in a man and C.D. showed up. He was intentional. He was clear, direct, and expressive. Just like I prayed. He spoke to things I had only shared with God in my silent prayer! He was the answer, right?!

Outside of that weird period of a week, we were good! At least from my perspective. I had no complaints. Not one! I loved this man. I had become very fond of his parents, talking with his mom regularly. I prayed for his children like I prayed for my own. I cooked for him! If you know me, then you know I *can* cook, I *will* cook, and I prefer *not* to cook. Real talk. The only time I cooked for a man, I was married to him – in the past! I loved serving C.D. It was natural. I saw my future with this man. Easily.

I started praying for his well-being and other areas of his life that I was inspired to cover in prayer. The dreams continued. I kept seeing his face, hearing his voice. I could not shake this man; I could not understand why!

From our playlist:
"Change on Me" by Xavier Omar

The Prompting

One morning, while praying, I was prompted to reach out to C.D. I was driving and almost had an accident when I heard and felt the prompt.

"Are you serious?" I asked God.

I pulled over to pray because this was an unusual prompting. I was trying to get over this man and move on with my life.

There is not an ex of mine in the world, dead or alive, who had a second chance with me. Their well-being was none of my concern after the breakup. Do you hear me? An ex is an ex, and I was never willing to even be friends with an ex.

I didn't want to look like a fool; however, I know that when God prompts me to do something my obedience is critical. So, I sent C.D. a text message. It was brief, respectful, and offered no indication of emotion.

I sent the text to be obedient. I sent it knowing that he was probably still asleep (if his work schedule had not changed). I was not expecting a response. I admit that my heart was hoping for one, however I had prepared myself to not hear anything back. Again, I was just trying to be obedient and move on.

I told C.D. early on that I would not stay where I did not feel welcomed or desired. I never want to be a burden to anyone. I would not fight for anyone who was not fighting for me. I would not go out of my way to prove my worth and value. I would not compete with other women, if that became the case. I was not an option, and this was not a game – hearts were on the line.

Had we remained friends that is different, yet he and I crossed the line into deep waters. Being *just* friends was not an option for us after our experience together.

A couple of hours passed after I sent the text. It was within the window of time that he usually wakes up that his name appeared on my screen. I was flushed with emotion. I was relieved, happy, and afraid. It took a few minutes before I opened the text to read it.

When I finally read the text, the glass wall I had built to protect my heart shattered instantly. Those suppressed feelings came to the surface and caused a flood in my eyes. My heart was exposed and wide open, again.

His message was respectful and kind. He said a lot, yet what penetrated was the part where he said that it was good to hear from me, he thinks about me often, he never intended for us to get to a place where we couldn't speak to each other, and he missed me.

HE MISSED ME!! My heart soaked every bit of that up. I thought it was just me with those feelings, so to learn that was not the case did something to me.

He attached a photo of us to his text. That did something to me, also. I had not been able to look at the thousands of photos we took. I captured as many moments as possible on camera. It was fun and we looked good together – very photogenic. Looking at the photo that he sent of the two of us was heartwarming. It brought back sweet memories and forced more tears down my cheeks.

I sat back in my car with tears in my eyes. I could no longer deny how much I missed him. I stared at our picture for a few minutes, as I allowed the gentle tears to fall down my face. I took a few slow, deep breaths. I prayed, then I replied. The door was now unlocked to communication and reconnecting.

***

Two weeks and two days later, we spent my birthday together. He arrived on my doorstep with flowers, a card, wine, and that smile. I opened the door and pushed all of that aside as I leaped into his arms.

Oh, my God! It felt so good to be in his arms again. He held me tight as we inhaled one another and planted kisses on each other's necks still locked in the embrace. We missed each other and it was evident.

That night after going out for my birthday, we held each other all night. We *just* held each other. No lie. Kissy faces and gentle touches. He would gently rub my face. I lovingly rubbed his bald head. We gazed into each other's eyes. We inhaled one another's scent and basked in each other's energy. We both took in the moment.

Lust was never a thing with us, and we shared intimacy on a different level. C.D. and I spent many nights together just grateful to be in each other's presence. There was nothing wrong with him or me, for that matter. In fact, early on he expressed how he didn't want to lead with sex, and he maintained that. What we cultivated was much deeper than physical and that was an answered prayer, too.

For the record, we are both attracted to one another, and our chemistry is on point. We just reached a place in life where focusing on what matters most became the priority. We shared this and agreed to it from the beginning

In addition to coming to see me on my birthday, we spent the day after my birthday together. We saw one another the following week, too.

We don't talk on the phone like we used to, for hours and hours, however we communicate regularly. We've had a few late night, long hour chats, too. Oh, the memories.

We haven't been visiting like we used to; however, we have expressed the desire to see one another and that will happen, I am sure. We understand business and responsibility come first. I think we're also being guarded and careful as we navigate what's in our hands. All in all, it's very clear that we care deeply and still have feelings for one another.

***

I have a profound love and respect for C.D. He received a different version of me than any other man. It was a new, healed version. I had my reservations and even experienced a few triggers in our relationship. There's no way of knowing what you need to work on until you are faced with it, right? We agreed to give one another what we had never given anyone else. I believe we did that.

We showed up for one another and we supported one another in countless ways. We shared in depth parts of ourselves with one another with the right motive and intent. We invested into the relationship, and we respect one another enough to be where we are.

I believe with every fiber in my being that we are meant to be in each other's lives. The depth and the capacity are still to be determined. I know that C.D. is an answer to my prayer, still. Sometimes the outcome of the prayer is not what we envision and sometimes it takes time for the vision to unfold. Either way, I am grateful for him. Again, he showed me something different and he gave me hope.

The way that I was prompted to reach out to him is of no credit to me. On my own, I would have never done it. I trust God, however, and I am grateful for my obedience and the results.

Reconnecting with C.D. provided me with healing that I was not aware was needed. I would have suppressed my true feelings for him and moved on. That's not healthy. Reconnecting with C.D. has matured me in a way I can't yet describe. It has added to my spiritual growth and given me a new perspective on many things.

Our journey was not an act or performance. We were both genuine from the beginning. I don't think we were completely ready for how fast things evolved, especially the feelings. Wisdom would teach us to slow down a bit, give it some time to take root. Genuine feelings don't just up and vanish, however, and love doesn't just go away.

I grew to a space of love for C.D. I did not fall in love. To *fall* is accidental and sometimes reckless. This was intentional. I made a choice to love him after observing him, spending time with him, and based on how he treated me. Our common and shared goals, beliefs and life philosophies also played a huge part. Our connection and level of comfort in each other's presence are a bonus. Those things don't necessarily mean you are supposed to be with a person, yet they serve as a pretty solid foundation to build from if you are supposed to be together.

At one point in the relationship with C.D., I prayed for a stronger and deeper connection between us. I prayed for a closer friendship. I think that is what's happening now.

I used to believe that it was not okay to be friends with an ex. I was wrong. I am not interested in befriending <u>any</u> other exes, not one bit, however C.D. is an exception. What we shared wasn't like anything I have ever experienced. What he showed me, what he taught me, etc., is unmatched.

My love and respect for C.D. outweigh that mystery week of questionable behavior and unanswered questions. The way that I still feel when I am with him is worth every bit of where we are today. I don't know what's ahead for us, yet I know that we have an affinity for one another. He's still the direct, expressive, and intentional man that I prayed for. He still makes me smile. He still makes me laugh. There's still *something about him*!!

From our playlist:
"Feelings" by Xavier Omar

LOVE NOTE #8

Dear C.D.,

Surprise! Happy Father's Day love! I hope this gift warms your heart and reminds you of how special you truly are to me. I still thank God for you. You are still my answered prayer and I appreciate you.

Thank you for being a stand-up man. Thank you for the journey we have shared and for taking the lead in the process. Thank you for "clearing the path" for me and for "choosing" me.

Although we are in a different space right now, I am simply grateful to still have you in my life. You brighten my days and I hope that I still brighten yours!

Thank you for taking your time with me. Thank you

for the nights you held me and just held me. Thank you for respecting me and for not lusting after me.

Thank you for supporting me... my goals, my dreams, and my endeavors. Thank you for supporting my children.

Thank you for reminding me to wash my feet (inside joke) and making sure that I eat. Thank you for checking on me, for your care, concern, and the many conversations we shared about anything and everything.

Thank you for trusting me and confiding in me. Thank you for valuing my input and opinion.

Thank you for introducing me to your world and sharing your family with me.

I honor you. Your self-control and self-discipline. Your growth and evolution. Your focus and determination. Your work ethic and business acumen. Your leadership and knack for responsibility. Your generosity and your respectability. Your spirit and your heart.

Thank you for your effort, investment, and involvement with our relationship, your family (and mine). Thank you for the advice you give that "they" may never thank you for. I see you and hear you. It's all from a place of love.

I am still on your side – right, wrong, or indifferent. And if you're wrong, I'll bring it to your attention privately and respectfully, and still stand next to you, cheering you on like a #1 fan! #teamCD

I honor you... as a father to your children and as a man. It's still #teamwin, King, for the long haul!

XOXO,
Luvface

From our playlist:
"Long Haul" by Conya Doss

"Sometimes love isn't planned.
It's stumbling upon someone,
feeling an instant connection,
and sharing a chemistry that
goes beyond understanding.

The most beautiful love
is the one you never saw coming
– a delightful surprise gifted by fate.
It's not about crossing fingers and hoping.
It's about those magical moments
where two hearts click effortlessly. Unexpected,
raw, and beautifully unplanned, true love is a
journey that starts
with an instant connection and grows
into something way beyond
what words can capture.

Embrace the unexpected,
for it often leads to the most profound
and fulfilling love stories."

From our playlist:
"First Time" by Teeks

www.ingramcontent.com/pod-product-compliance
Lightning Source LLC
LaVergne TN
LVHW090534110826
845146LV00003B/1092